The Life and Work of
Paul Cézanne

Sean Connolly

Heinemann
LIBRARY

www.heinemann.co.uk/library
Visit our website to find out more information about **Heinemann Library** books.

To order:
 Phone 44 (0) 1865 888066
 Send a fax to 44 (0) 1865 314091
 Visit the Heinemann Bookshop at www.heinemann.co.uk/library to browse our catalogue and order online.

First published in Great Britain by Heinemann Library, Halley Court, Jordan Hill, Oxford OX2 8EJ, part of Harcourt Education.
Heinemann is a registered trademark of Harcourt Education Ltd.

Editorial: Clare Lewis
Design: Jo Hinton-Malivoire and Q2A Creative
Illustrations by Karin Littlewood
Production: Helen McCreath

Printed and bound in China by South China Printing Company

10 digit ISBN 0 431 09885 9
13 digit ISBN 978 0 431 09885 2

10 09 08 07 06
10 9 8 7 6 5 4 3 2 1

British Library Cataloguing in Publication Data
Connolly, Sean
The Life and Work of: Paul Cézanne
759.4
A full catalogue record for this book is available from the British Library.

Acknowledgements
The publishers would like to thank the following for permission to reproduce photographs:
Page 4, Portrait photograph of Paul Cézanne, 1889, Credit: AKG. Page 5, Paul Cézanne Self-Portrait with beret, Credit: B & U International Picture Service. Page 7, Paul Cézanne 'Sketchbook studies', Credit: R.M.N/Michele Bellot. Page 9, Paul Cézanne Paul Alexis reading to Emile Zola, Credit: Giraudon. Page 11, Paul Cézanne Portrait of Pissarro, Credit: Giraudon. Page 12, Boulevard des Capucines, Credit: Hulton Getty. Page 13, Paul Cézanne Landscape, Auvers, Credit: Philadelphia Museum of Art. Page 15, Paul Cézanne L'Etang des Sœurs, Orsy, Credit: Courtauld Institute. Page 17, Paul Cézanne The Blue Vase, Credit: Giraudon. Page 19, Paul Cézanne The Pool at the Jas de Bouffan, Credit: Metropolitan Museum of Art. Page 21, Paul Cézanne The Card Players, Credit: The Bridgeman Art Library/Metropolitan Museum of Art. Page 23, Paul Cézanne La Montagne Sainte-Victoire, Credit: National Gallery of Scotland. Page 25, Paul Cézanne Portrait of Ambroise Vollard, Credit: Giraudon. Page 26, Mont Sainte-Victoire, Credit: Corbis. Page 27, Paul Cézanne Mont Sainte-Victoire, Credit: Philadelphia Museum of Art. Page 28, Portrait photograph of Cézanne in front of the picture Grand Bathers, Credit: Giraudon. Page 29, Paul Cézanne En Batau, Credit: National Museum of Western Art, Tokyo.

Cover photograph of L'oncle Dominique en avocat (Uncle Dominique as lawyer) by Paul Cézanne, reproduced with permission of The Art Archive / Musee d'Orsay Paris / Dagli Orti.

The publishers would like to thank Nancy Harris for her assistance in the preparation of this book.

Every effort has been made to contact copyright holders of any material reproduced in this book. Any omissions will be rectified in subsequent printings if notice is given to the publishers.

The paper used to print this book comes from sustainable resources.

Some words in the book are bold, **like this**. You can find out what they mean by looking in the Glossary.

Contents

Who was Paul Cézanne? 4

Early years 6

Life in Paris 8

Swapping ideas 10

Brush with fame 12

Ideas of his own 14

Between two worlds 16

New freedom 18

Ordinary people 20

Southern sunshine 22

Turning to people 24

A favourite view 26

Cézanne's last years 28

Timeline 30

Glossary 31

More books to read and paintings to see 31

Index 32

Who was Paul Cézanne?

Paul Cézanne was a painter. He used colours and shapes to paint pictures of nature. He helped change the way artists look at things and paint them.

Cézanne painted this **portrait** of himself
when he was about 60 years old.
A portrait is a picture of a person.

Early years

Paul Cézanne was born on 19 January 1839 in Aix-en-Provence, France. One of his childhood friends was called Emile Zola. The boys loved to hike in the countryside.

Paul **studied** drawing when he was a teenager. He often drew pictures on his walks in the country. This drawing shows that he was interested in nature.

Life in Paris

Paul wanted to be an artist. When he was 22 years old, his father gave him some money. He moved to Paris to be a painter.

Paul's friend Emile Zola had become a famous writer in Paris. He liked Paul's work and told other people about it. This painting shows a friend of Paul's reading to Emile.

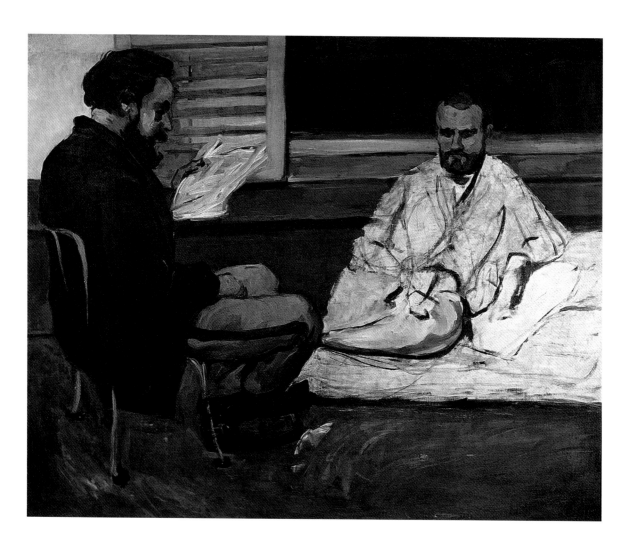

Swapping ideas

In Paris, Paul became very friendly with a painter called Camille Pissarro. They would go to Camille's country house, to paint outside. These trips reminded Paul of home.

Paul did this **sketch** of Camille Pissarro in 1874. It shows how the painters would pack their things and hike to a favourite spot to paint.

Brush with fame

A group of painters called the **Impressionists** liked Paul's paintings. They painted colourful pictures, too. They showed two of Paul's paintings at their first **exhibition** in 1874. The exhibition was in a building in this street in Paris.

This **landscape** from the exhibition shows how Paul used strong colours. The patches of light and dark help to show the shape of the houses.

Ideas of his own

Paul began to try different ways of painting. Patterns of colour and shape were more important to Paul than exact copies of a **scene**.

Paul did this painting when he was 38 years old. It uses thick, rough patches of paint to show how he saw a woodland pond.

Between two worlds

Paul also **studied** the work of the great artists of the past. He liked the French and Dutch artists who had lived more than 200 years before him.

The artists of the past had loved **still life** painting. Paul's painting of a blue vase shows that he loved it in the same way.

New freedom

Paul's father died in 1886 and Paul **inherited** enough money to live well. Now he did not have to worry about whether people would buy his paintings or not.

This meant Paul was now free to use new ways of painting. This **landscape** uses small blocks of colour to build a picture.

Ordinary people

Even though he was rich, Paul still thought
of himself as ordinary. He painted other
ordinary people and used his ideas about
colour and shape.

This is one of many pictures Paul painted of card players. Although he was painting people, Paul saw the **scene** as a pattern of colours.

Southern sunshine

Paul began to spend more time near his childhood home. He **studied** the way the sun changed the colour of the countryside.

Paul liked to paint a mountain called Mont Sainte-Victoire. This painting shows how he used colour to show distance as well as shapes.

Turning to people

Ambroise Vollard was an **art dealer** in Paris. He had a successful **exhibition** of Paul's paintings in 1895. At the same time Paul began work on some **portraits**.

This is a portrait of Ambroise Vollard. Paul worked hard on each painting. He never finished this one, even though Ambroise had to **pose** for it 115 times!

A favourite view

Paul still worked mainly in the south of France. He painted Mont Sainte-Victoire to show his ideas about colour, light, and shape.

This view of the mountain in 1904 shows
how Paul's work had changed. The
mountain has become just a **blurred**
pattern of colour.

Cézanne's last years

As he grew old, Paul still painted. He even ordered new paintbrushes just before he died in 1906, aged 67. By this time people knew he was a great painter.

In 1905 Paul did this painting of a group
of people. He used **watercolour** paints.
This type of painting was less tiring for
Paul as he got older.

Timeline

1839   Paul Cézanne is born in Aix-en-Provence, France on 19 January.

1861   Paul moves to Paris to become a painter.

1860s   Paul learns more about painting from his friend Camille Pissarro.

1871   Paul begins to paint outside to see light and colour more clearly.

1874   Paul has two paintings shown in the first **Impressionist Exhibition**.

1886   Paul's father dies.

1895   Ambroise Vollard sets up a one-man exhibition of Paul's paintings.

1902   Paul builds a new studio to view Mont Saint-Victoire.

1906   Paul Cézanne dies in Aix-en-Provence on 22 October.

Glossary

art dealer someone who sells paintings

blur unclear or fuzzy

exhibition public showing of paintings

Impressionists group of artists who painted freely, showing light and movement

inherit receive money when someone dies

landscape painting of the countryside

portrait painting of a person

pose to sit or stand still while being drawn

scene place or area

sketch another word for a drawing

still life painting of things that are on a table

study learn about a subject

watercolour type of paint that is mixed with water and can be used quickly

More books to read

The Children's Book of Art, Rosie Dickens (Usborne Publishing, 2005)

More paintings to see

Zola's House, Paul Cézanne, Burrell Collection, Glasgow

Still Life with Water Jug, Paul Cézanne, Tate Gallery, London

The Gardener Vallier, Paul Cézanne, Tate Gallery, London

Index

Aix-en-Provence 6

birth 6

death 28

Impressionists 12

Mont Sainte-Victoire 23, 26, 27

Paris 8, 9, 10, 12

Pissarro, Camille 10, 11

Vollard, Ambroise 24, 25

Zola, Emile 6, 9